I0457683

CALL ME
EARTHLING

Crooked Treehouse Press
&
Hook Love Books

Copyright © 2022-2023 Terry Blade

All Rights Reserved.

ISBN: 978-1-961461-09-3

All Words, Images, And Design By
Terry Blade

Introduction

Somehow I poked my nose out from behind the curtain. Between the strange incantations, theatrical plumes of smoke, far too many dust storms that thankfully didn't turn into tornadoes, I birthed this small manuscript. I had been wandering, always near the edge of survival, and certainly not writing more than a few lines of poetry for at least sixteen years as of spring 2022.

Most of that story is for another day, though some aspects of those years of my journey are here, either spelled out explicitly or permeating every fiber of each page. When my health and life met the sledgehammer, I had no place left to stand. I found no solid ground except what I created from sheer stubbornness, and a fistful of shards, remains of privilege from my previous life, some from a career that had come to an abrupt end over five years before. Also I must credit a handful of kind souls in this sphere and beyond.

Each word is a burnt offering voiced through a burnt offering.

These poems were written in 2022. A few have roots, a title or perhaps a refrain, that reaches back to lost work from the early 2000s. Though I tried, I never managed to write in form before 2022. My brain operates much differently now though a substantial portion of my perception of this world remains. So it is that this book contains a mixture of both form and free verse.

Any adventures described that may have occurred during my years of wandering came at a cost, whether by my choice or forced upon me by circumstance. The lessons of a life come at a steep price. Hopefully we learn to hold them dear.

CALL ME EARTHLING

Who Bore Me..1
Before Waking...2
My Name Was Never Tommy...4
Part of the Truth about Labor Day Weekend 1979.......................6
Skidmarked...10
1979...12
Not A Ploy...14
Reverberation...16
Solid...17
In The Light...18
Dyke Night...19
Forbidden...20
Mitts to Hit..22
Dating While Homeless...24
Gulf of California..25
HyperReactive...26
Old Mojo...28
Up to my Neck...30
Ghosting a Rando..32
After Life Suspended...36
Desert Waking...39
Does Genital Electrolysis Qualify as a Haircut.........................40
My Fused Closed Cunt Was A No-Vagina Monologue...............42
Birdsongs (Illusion of Dawn)..46
Could Even Kill...47
Incubation...50
Shelter...52
In My Dreams (after The Dark's song Judy II)..........................54
What Needs To Change..56
Hard Land..58
Cutout..60
Graffiti 61

Who Bore Me

Lawn Madonnas tremble as I walk the street
Sidewalk opens like a cave
She bore Jesus but who bore me

Draw bitter stares from all I meet
Shattered spirit none can save
Lawn Madonnas tremble as I walk the street

Neighbors vanish not to meet
My gaze perhaps would make them rave
She bore Jesus but who bore me

I see all this, they're not discreet
I give the distance we all crave
Lawn Madonnas tremble as I walk the street

Downward spiral of concrete
My insane world not flat, concave
She bore Jesus but who bore me

May be that I concede defeat
And hasten my way to the grave
Lawn Madonnas tremble as I walk the street
She bore Jesus but who bore me

Before Waking

In time before waking, liminal space
I recall it was you I once adored
My mind does a dance, steps retrace
To my life that I feared to explore

I recall it was you I once adored
Though today I live uncomfortably numb
To my life that I feared to explore
Error message, nostalgia succumb

Though today I live uncomfortably numb
In dreamscape I cannot escape
Error message, nostalgia succumb
Too many reasons, I felt so unsafe

In dreamscape I cannot escape
No person would I could trust
Too many reasons, I felt so unsafe
So I bolted, smoke and dust

No person would I could trust
Trust in life was the ultimate cost
So I bolted, smoke and dust
Not comprehending what I had lost

Trust in life was the ultimate cost
For I had nowhere to turn
Not comprehending what I had lost
I was the only bridge left to burn

For I had nowhere to turn
Surrounded, my life lived in fright
I was the only bridge left to burn
No way out, no horizon in sight

Surrounded, my life lived in fright
Now haunting the borders of sleep, your face
No way out, no horizon in sight
Decades passed, seasons offer no grace

Now haunting the borders of sleep, your face
My mind does a dance, steps retrace
Decades passed, seasons offer no grace
In time before waking, liminal space

My Name Was Never Tommy
But Maybe Pinball Saved My Life

At the Circle
where a large beer boilermaker
was a buck
and you could bring your dog
most of the bikers
had lost their rides
to dope men's friends

I sat alone in a slab built booth
when I wasn't pounding
at the bar

Inside the clatter of
weathered and checked
wood screen doors
I never tried
to bluff my way
out of a fight

These folks were not
blustering townies
down the street
made slow by slabs of lasagne
and bad cover bands

I never saw the rental rooms upstairs
There was only one way out
besides a window

If I thought about it
I may have named that narrow stairway
that emptied next to the juke box
the most dangerous place in town

But I was chasing amnesia too hard
to let language shackle instinct
so my foot never fell upon that first step
and my face did not know the feel of
well worn boards, sawdust, and ashes

No sucker punch
Nor coldcock
For a sodden wraith
From another place

I left early to coax games
From already ancient arcade machines
more often than I saw last call

Part of the Truth about Labor Day Weekend 1979

I was perc loaded. That was my night time baseline. That was the only way I could stay vertical, never mind dance, without a clenched jaw and those quick sharp inhalations that announced each lightning bolt shot down my right leg. Underneath it all, was the perpetual dull-ache backing track, a drone that came to stay, along with jagged bolts toothed with electric silver. Two years since the tanker truck rear ended me on 128. Two years of this crap, and I needed back surgery, bad.

My friends had drifted off, maybe to the narrow part of one of the dance floors. Nancy liked to dance with gay boys, and I think her boyfriend Joe liked to watch, though he would never admit it. The Twelve was the best place for that. I had few choices in town since I certainly wasn't going to be welcomed in the usual dyke hangouts.

There had been no women around earlier, so I danced with three buff and tanned boys. Round and round, back to front, in a ritual whose home was a grassy clearing on the first night of spring as much as it was this upstairs dance floor at summer's end. This was the weekend of U-Hauls, Comm Ave traffic jams, and first cruises on the Fenway. The air was still hot out on the concrete sidewalk, like I want to lick that ice cream chill as it begins to run over corrugations, course of sweet sticky rivers tracing chocolate chip outlines of my finger tips.

One boy took off his tight fitting ribbed tank and swung it toward the back of another. I stepped aside and continued to dance with the circle that was forming around the young men, who were now all shirtless and mock-flogging each other to the pulse of the music. I half wished I was into guys.

Then somehow, I was downstairs leaning on the big bar with another drink in my hand, because I could never swallow enough oblivion and make it bond to my being for more than a breath or two. My heart was always beating. Its intrusive, rhythmically boring vibration like my landlord's kids' too loud Pink Floyd rippling through the walls up to my attic apartment. And with all these things came that reminder to breathe. I hated to think about breathing, nor about the burden of expanding my ribcage, as I took another pull from yet another cigarette. I killed the drink.

There had been that underlying ripple of excitement. Maybe it was the edge of prescience. Maybe it was simply the feeling of possibility resurrected through the magic of a three day weekend, a wad of cash in my pockets, and a combination of drugs and booze that was almost working.

The dance floor on this level was more open and the air less close. There was more space, and the colored lights played over the dancers so that they stood out as individuals rather than an undifferentiated sea of movement. That ceaseless writhing flesh ritual of dance continued upstairs, but here there was crispness, edges restored, a blast of air conditioning directly on my face and head

And there she was. There are never any better words for that moment. Silver sparkle over black. Tall and moving like curvy but sinuous priestess, like she dreamed that dance a thousand times, like she owned it since before this lifetime, like her smile alone had created this, jump started the seed of movement from stagnancy and so began this world. I mouthed only two words as I was drawn to join her Yes. This.

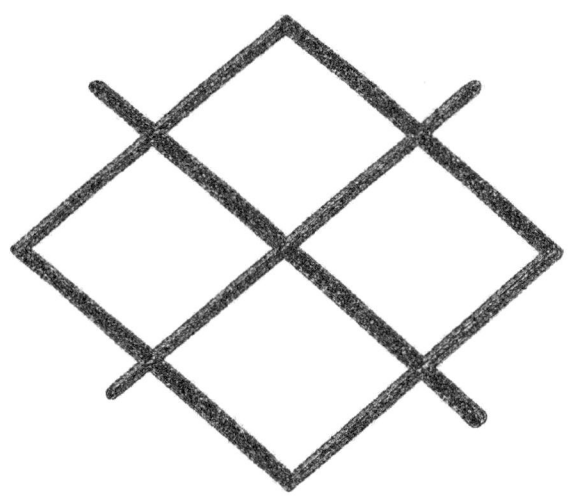

SKIDMARKED

Dad paraded in skidmarked tighty whiteys
But put on pants for company
When he wasn't trying to convince me
to love my dick
By waving his like it's flag day
While Mom cursed out my man-hating girlfriend
This is my kitchen, and that's my ironing board

Should I have tossed that ironing board
Perhaps punched Dad in the eyes of his whitey
Too self centered to have a girlfriend
But at my apartment, she was not company
When I woke next to her, that first day
I certainly didn't know dick

People who think its all about dick
They need to be laid out, pinned to a board
And left to ponder for a day
Sunbleached wood, sunburned whitey
Alone, no company
No waifu, no girlfriend

No girlfriend
For you, Dick
Go work for the company
Who cares, be elected to the board
Go blend in, is that skin whitey or mobster Whitey
Or is it both, all day every day

Not your liberation day
I'm not your bolt cutter wielding girlfriend
Not your cunt pink whitey
Let go your dick
You ain't hardwood, you ain't board
You're not worth bad company

You don't know, to stroke company
That it all hinges on the day
On feel, grain of the board
Don't be hating girlfriend
Or a crazy-assed dick
You're stuck with whitey

Time for company, Ironing Board
No dad, no skidmarked, whitey perhaps less day
I'll stay with man-hating girlfriend,
dad can keep his dick

1979

We wandered Fenway streets
after last call
In never-ending quest for my
1964 Riviera
and perhaps my friends who needed a ride home
Or should I say on a long overdue
search and rescue mission for ourselves
Over pavement, under streetlights
Telephone lines cast shadows of abandoned ski lifts
while drunken humans bobbed in the current
Tides driven by traffic
Four lanes to Chinatown or to my suburban attic
A bed, a table, a second hand couch

Where had I buried the briefcase this time?
In the Riviera's trunk?
Next to my bed while I did not sleep?
They stole my pillow case last time
and anything they felt moved to stuff into it
I caught a different thief who had smashed the Riv's dash
out of sheer ignorance
before running off across a parking lot in Lowell
Would they steal you lying next to me?

Would that they stole my secrets
unseen which sundered us and
left me lost to those who came before
Chop-shop my coachwork, leave me bareboned

The Rivieras had an X-shaped frame
that would snap in half upon application of lateral forces
such as from a tree or another vehicle
There was no protection for the passengers
from a perpendicular or oblique impact

You struck me with insufficient force
Kinetic of joyriding each other's life
But it's a lie to say
that I simply read that wrong
in my denial of our sentimental selves
Lacking knowledge of
where you were weak or strong
nor how to strip my own stubborn exoskeleton
I only felt that last act
would be purely suicidal
in 1979

Not A Ploy

When I called you from my cousin's wedding
Asking to come to the apartment
Where we had once lived
Together but apart, each alone
I genuinely was too wasted
It was not manipulation

You always used manipulation
Your eyes, lighthouses that pulsed wedding
Work and school, my time was not wasted
In my room, basement apartment
In my pain, alone
Somehow I lived

When you lived
At you mother's,
your hands and mouth felt less a manipulation
On your waterbed, after our storm,
sometimes I felt less alone
But never wedding, never my terror, wedding
Rather marry my own room,
and my weed, in our apartment
Rather stay camouflaged, and wasted

That night I sprawled in your chair on wheels, wasted
The universe revolved in the room where you still lived
Where springtime's river
had rolled through our old apartment
When you pulled down my pants,
I struggled to know if it was manipulation
Check compass and genuflect toward wedding
Or did you simply want to spend time together alone

Your singular mouth alone
My springtime's river vomited wasted
Into trash basket, our ceremony, wedding
Perhaps a fragment of some dream died, that had lived
No manipulation
I'd only wanted to crash in our old apartment

Was it cursed, that apartment
Or were we, each alone
Targets of cosmic manipulation
Wandering comet crashed down energy wasted
Smoking crater where we once lived
Extinction event, wedding

Manipulation, to the windows, flooded our apartment
Wedding to myself alone
In those years, I lived hidden and wasted

REVERBERATION

While I craved silence in my cubby
A neverending cocaine fueled fuck
and Jerry's wanking solos
at four AM did reverberate
every blessed morning
above my head

Solid

Slick syringe barrel slides between my fingers
former home of crinkled paper
Ten thousand Marlboros extracted from red and white
printed cardboard
where naphtha scented wick nestled next to
caress of thumb wheel and flint
Needle, hollow point freed from blaze orange
is always poised to penetrate
membrane, muscle, or a quick pinch
The way a thumb and forefinger grab up a bit of human
Homing for blood
Sliding like smoke of those Marlboros penetrated alveoli
Every yearning to get inside can be held between two
outstretched fingers or a sigh
The way mouth takes polished steel barb
So many ways to taste iron and tears
in lifetimes lived like catch and release
Burble of river eddies
Foaming backs of water's snakes
where rainbows run above Jemez
that the people call Walatowa
Before black ice and sand signal an end to a season's hunt
When a voice calls across the room
lights flickering off and on
Or the door groans and clicks behind
Them
Thumb on slick plunger seeks home
Finds bottom
The solid feel of an ending

In The Light

I pray to those who I may or may not believe in
Whose marks are carried in my flesh and memory
That the Karma and Reincarnation you profess,
are in fact true
That in your reconstituted form
you may again walk this world
bereft of your priestly robes,
your doubletalk, and your dick

Sleazebag
Meanwhile you flaunt victimhood
like every spotlight is yours to claim
Have them
dogging and capturing your every plea and gesticulation
Parade and strut in your arrogance
Dance for us

DYKE NIGHT

She wanted to get Jack
She danced with me
I told her about Jack

She was hot
Jack was hot
I was old
and I was not
But she danced with me
a lot

I was a pariah
who never got laid
Did it matter
Sex made me feel
my deepest longings
for death

So she got with Jack
and made art with Jack
And still
sometimes danced with me
while I made art with death

Forbidden

I am that which was forbidden
lost one from a younger world
Stumbling way toward sacredness
Taking blows, midst of assault
What is the dance, what is my dance
Must I always spin alone

I was told to stand alone
the thought of other ways forbidden
Round edges of a neighborhood,
I forced myself to dance
Compress to fit a shrunken world
Would that protect me from assault
and help me seek my sacredness

Their plan, to strip my sacredness
to leave me bare-skinned and alone
From neighborhood I thought my own,
the same old dastardly assault
It mattered not the tone,
my every word forbidden
by spirit of a broken world
My bleeding feet, no place to dance

So in my dreams, I then did dance
in sanctuary sacredness
While passing time, and spinning world
left me in the dust, alone
Thought police still shout, Forbidden
though more distant their assault

Torches of assault
light my pathway, when I dance
when I show my ways, forbidden
Their disregard for sacredness
let that be theirs alone
Forever banished from my world

I spin my world
and skirt assault
This victory alone
Is My Dance
In living way of sacredness
For I am that which was forbidden

Alone in this world
I lived forbidden, under assault
I learned my dance,
and found my home in sacredness

Mitts to Hit

Hot blitz
Hot mitts
Mitts grabbed for me
Mitts grabbed for my tits
Tits she tweaked
Tits she disappointed
Disappointed tweak not hot
Disappointed there's no question
Question is she dork
Question of temperature
Temperature rising
Temperature is fever
Fever brings chills
Fever means horny
Horny makes people insane
Horny makes people play games
Games escape me I'm too old
Games protect me you're too cold
Cold forgotten in the heat
Cold feet you won't go down
Down for the thickness
Down for my thigh
Thigh ain't chicken
Thigh is why

Why are you to me so cold
Why so icy when you're hot
Hot confuse me
Hot I'm not
Not get hit on
Not a robot
Robot sex is in your dreams
Robot Asimov obsession
Obsession Josephson erection
Obsession masturbation session
Session breaks Hitachi
Session breaks into tears
Tears are proxy
Tears for fears
Fears of shadow
Fears of self
Self do you want to bang an elf
Self is merciless
Merciless sad
Merciless ruler
Ruler hits
Ruler hit
Hit me
Hit me
Hit me

Dating While Homeless

We made out
leaning on the old van I'd painted with a brush
I always picked up the tab for food
before going out for public lewd
Us just bring human, no big crush
No future plan, no big rush
Simply unconcealed, and swollen, our ending a prelude
Luxury of my station, do you think it crude?
Do you blush? No, my life was not plush

For cattle road, and dust were my home
My haven, mind and body broken
Most safe refuge, far from pavement,
was still downright dangerous
Days and weeks and years alone
Volumes of my life, still unspoken
Reasons to go on are not painless

Gulf of California

Tonight's wind is from Puerto Peñasco

Warm and damp Gulf of California
rolls over the desert
like a long-ago broken wave, nearly spent

Bubbles, ripples, a bit of rain to waken
memories held within fossil sea snails and
trilobites

Jumbled rocks on a hillside where cattle forage
above a dry riverbed

HyperReactive

My mistake was survival
The error of any way every way

            Soap for my sick body
            made by a sick man in his basement
            until it wasn't
            because it went bad
            Bad basement

Time measured in soap bubbles,
sunburn, and frostbite
Time measured in currency
Time measured in cunt stitches and kenalog
Time measured in lines on syringes
The tick graduated in bong hits and benzedrine

            Life without squeeze toy ducks
            a main squeeze
            or any squeeze as such

The wrong end of too many muzzles
and too little chill

I never thought I'd ever live in a van
back when weed man
swung his sawed off out of paper bag
back of his van

Paper bags blow away in wind
Dust storms dissect me
My life was only half a pound

In paranoia of the day
security was paramount

When the feds took my acquaintances
they left my small time ass behind
while the rest sold each other out
hoping for a break

Old Mojo

The last thing I want is my old mojo back
I was the friendly pariah
not at all the life of the party
A novel once christened me broken in my sex
Men approached my child self in the day and in the dark
I began weak but decades made me strong

How do you show a bully that you are strong
Once you leave them behind, there is no going back
Old and weak, on hot nights I fear the dark
Except when I am the asshole pariah
Many say you can't change it but what the fuck is sex
I hung with the host's dog at the play party

I rarely played at the party
How do I show myself that I am strong
wondering if I would ever again have sex
Back to parking lot makeouts, back to back
Should I have got the tattoo, "Pariah"
I drove off the cattle road after the party,
nodding and creeping in the dark

I jot down new theologies in the dark
Vacant grownup children at the party
A homemade mask can't hide the queer pariah
I was always running, only my legs were strong
But also always running back
If climax rendered you broken for weeks,
would you fear sex

When I kept my pants on,
the neighbors could still hear our sex
There is also a place of comfort, stroking terror,
who am I hiding from in the dark
Only one ex ever wanted me back
I was bloody pincushion
when the cops showed up at the party
It was my stubbornness that somehow made me strong
They can't hide the hurt pariah

Family tranny-girl pariah
Freud needs to sit on his cigar,
trade his cocaine for sex
How do I come back from death's door,
when only my middle finger stands strong
and summer's Sunday morning hammer, shatters the dark
Perhaps a miracle, I remained sober at the party
Long nights, starless and bible black,
dawn always roars back

Sonoran wilds shaped me, strong pariah
Back, sex, back! I'm back to badlands
Slipping into morning dark,
party in desert city was not my home

Up to my Neck

1
Flesh hooks and skewers don't scare me
near as much as you all
Gloves and masks
Buttressed against unruly flesh
Human stew, the contents of condoms
and coatings of cast off gauntlets strewn across
orderly grids of victory gardens

Every party a parting gesture
and calculation
Degrees of separation
roll back and forth through cranial cavities
Empty bottles of poppers
bouncing through guttersheen puddles

We are all driven by thunderstorm
and rationalization
The ways that
fingertips desperately claw for purchase on cliffs edge
Huddled and wrapped in premeditated rebuttal
Hollow sound of ice against glass in a barkeep's hand
Scalpel drops into red plastic container
The laughable squeek of too much new black leather
Too many ways to stiffen a body

2

It's always easier to get someone off good
if they repulse me
The slightest glimmer of like beyond the abstract
or generalized good will can
tangle neurons
Lust is a cheap marlinspike
that snaps when you lean on it
Voids in my superstructure
remained mystery shrouded in black or blue denim

3

I retch
Not from her gutter breath
But stubble brings thoughts of my father
What one thing on any given night
may tripline me onto impaling spikes
I gasp and reach to explore
joys of her testosterone nourished clit

4

If it's not forbidden
why bother
When stigma killing
is a funeral for pleasure
I can only attempt to lean on laughter
In name of new and improved
I Never spit on the children

Ghosting a Rando

I made more tea
Retrieved the remains
of my take-out portion
from frigidare jumble
Ate to a soundtrack of
her bellysleep snores
tick of wall clock
woosh of swamp cooler
The dog was finally quiet

I did not hurry
as I set clean plates
on the rack
gave
stainless basin
a finishing rub

All the hemp
and jute hanks,
black hide mitts
with their shackles
locks and keys,
Thuddy Flogger,
and Big D
I bagged each
with care
Placed all in a courier's sack
I retrieved from the end zip
of my olive-drab duffel

Mainspring winds down
from the moment
we meet
Service topping isn't always that way
But I was ready

My longing rose
for groaning hinges
throw of deadbolt
Tomorrow morning
I would finger the block button
on a tiny screen

She knew that
but pretended
not to hear

There are reasons
I am terrified
by mummification
by cling wrap
by mayonnaise in any context

I hoped to vanish
fade like a wraith
into brightening sunrise
to be over

But her ill-tempered Chihuahua
who fancied himself Xolotl
seemed prepared to rain
heavenly fire upon me
Spitting, Snarling
How did that diminutive creature
simultaneously levitate and spin
blocking the door to the walkway

My egress was prevented
not only by that
four-legged psychopath
but by my better self
Keyless, I could not secure the entry

I had no choice but to rouse
the naked and benumbed bed dweller
and make her complicit
in my escape

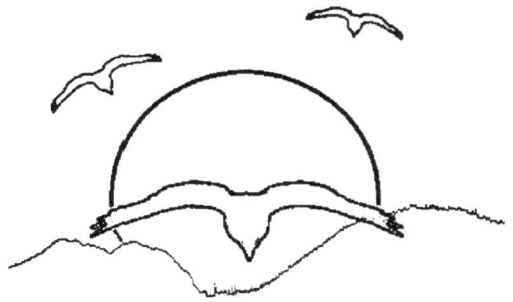

AFTER LIFE SUSPENDED

Help me if you can
to not run the light
to not nod off
There's a cop
corner of Pecos and Arizona Ave at 3:39AM
Turn left
to float south on a ribbon
created by my motion
through fields sprayed damp in circles
Pungent with green and fusarium
I breathe my way
to Casa Grande
supercenter tarmac

There my runes
Intent and devotion
writ that day in pen and gentian violet
frighten off a rag-tag vanload of sober evangelists
My chosen form of space clearing
display forearms and fists
against tide of holy rolling squadron
Smile as they drive off heads shaking
semaphore of their
shared sense of certainty

Hook holes are oozing
all down my body's front
I choose my stigmata
My miracles performed by mortal hands
Sometimes this is how we spell family
in a different birthing ward

My old steroid-weakened collagen hide
never strong enough
to fight Earth's clutches for long
"Gravity pulls my face
pulls my skin"
A bit of suture
stitches together my
nothing but memories

You all flew like angels
triumphantly wounded
My pride in everyone else
while everlong questioning myself

I am checked and weather worn driftwood
unrecognized remains
rolling on shoreline of shut-eye
still hearing music's echos
There are places in me
born to reverberate

Vision of rig lines
glint of chain links and eyebolts
captured in crisscross of spotlights above
before I turned to blindfold
Turned in and outward
Turned on a swivel
Turned into offering

Shut-eye shut-eye shut-eye
and drift a bit
on the edge of recall
That searing returns
as I slowly spin
before daystar's hammer slaps my van
roasts me into parched waking
Consecrated broiler where I nightly toss and turn
Dream
Now

Desert Waking

I smell of funk and texas oil field towns
against the damp creosote bush and sage of this
rainy desert

My ears ring spiral seashells
like the last bit of a wave's spent power
rolling over wet sand
toward a moment of motionless empty
Again and again

There is breath
There are the rivers in me and
scar that speaks in erogenous bonesong harmonies

There is chill drifting over this skin
and still the waves sing their last moments to me
always ending, always spent

There are prayers wound through all of this
voices of orbit and a billion pilgrims
tide and the way a desert wind tears at every edge
eventually topples all who are too weak
or simply makes us one with the sweetness of its dust

Does Genital Electrolysis Qualify as a Haircut
~ or ~
Woman, That's Quite the Mullet You Have There

Barbed wire Jesus was savior
in the moldy room, where crotches she probed
Methodical and measured, would she fulfill hopes
of a pussy that someone, someday may savor
Christ in every direction, on barbed wire cross,
would she find his favor
Coils of metal, to hold him, no ropes
No hope, this depiction, of approval by popes
But her work by surgeons, said to be raver
for the woman who seeks brand new cherry flavor

To her shower first, to wash off the homeless
Heat of Phoenix summer so hard
Then with needle, follicles she charred
Few I could tell, who may condone this
Conversation with all my family barred
of my decades long quest, in the end to be boneless

My Fused Closed Cunt Was A No-Vagina Monologue

When afterglow merged
with self assured destruction
phased into solid
unyielding substance
Dross cast upon
Philosopher's Stone

You called me to be your token
when few doors were open
Starving women flocked to feed
with tales of their mega-clits
odes to daddy surgeons

I refused

He knelt before me
moustached, squinting
Cue David Lee
singing Panama

As I sprawled in a hotel chair of
cotton candy marshmallow,
blue gloved hand
reached shrunken
but persistently protruding
grief

Like an auditor
turning pages
over and back
scanning for signs
of attempts at erasure
he was
perhaps
perplexed

Endurance is
my most strong shield

Cue
If I cling to the piling of this mattress
swirling currents cannot
drag me in to darkness

Cue
Unmoving arms will not empty me red

Cue
This how to live poorly
to stash dollars

Cue
But this is how to binge on toys
and blow it all away

Cue
Cut rate flights and cheap hotels

Cue
More volleys
Snap
of needle blast

Cue
Learn to love
the smell of burning keratin
In the morning

Cue
Strategic lies

Cue
Subvert the gatekeepers

My playlist
Is not your hearts and flowers day gift

My playlist
Is not for your audience's crossed legged pleasure

My playlist
Is not your trial

My playlist
Is mine

I test sutures in my stubborn body
who refuses this world
Thread curved needles
through my thigh
Bind skin in sloppy surgeon's knots
Create a hodgepodge of welts, scabs, and scars
My miniature
road to freedom
cratered and speedbumped
with hope

He edged back
Knot crowning his wire frames
grew
as he met my gaze
and said
I think there may be just enough

Birdsongs (Illusion of Dawn)

Lightening sky begs me
to accept the illusion of one more day
How can one prepare
for such a bombardment
Might my fist
if my arm were of sufficient length
knock this sky back into welcome darkness
send singing birds back to rest

Earlier, I pined for my former home
made mostly of memory within myself
I am nothing but creature of shadow
veneer of dust
that falls to line tiny rivulets
of cooling raindrops

Could Even Kill

Years, are these the best you got

Desert heat
Dusty grit in teeth
Heart labors ceaselessly
Flee that which weighs you down

Hurt will stop you dead
Hurt will strand you in a land
that births
only life with spikes

Desert vellum, sweat and dust
Flee those who only hurt
leave dusty scars upon ones heart

Years, the seasons flee
Fire and ice sheet finery
while marrow grows heavy
with every gallon I haul

Heart once broken rarely heals
This burden shattered my pride
crossing infinite drywash
until I finally befriended
Sage, Creosote, Yerba Santa
Cows, and Coyote

A dustbound brain in heat thinks slow
If I tell you
flee the thought police
those who live for the imprisonment
of your self
will you leave them behind
or perhaps smile as
you cast them out of your abyss

Flee the arrows of your hurt
heart pacing through years
or turn and snatch them
like Shaolin or Jedi
of this place where
coal train's rumble
is your sonar 10 miles out

Heart of the matter is heart
as years fold in on each other
and wind-borne grit spreads over life

Dusty roads wash out in storms
What seems like no escape
is simply the way that water
hitch hikes
No se necesita pasaporte
when the monsoon driven Tanque Verde
blasts into town like instant rapids
surfed southeast wind
over smoking mountain peaks

One October in another life
I watched the people break into dance
singing Mayim! Mayim! Mayim!
as clouds burst open above Jerusalem

But dusty love still can't find a heart
Not now
not in the past I sometimes flee
That hurt could even kill the desert
when heart of the matter is years
and desolate voices crackle dusty
on new moon nights

Incubation

I feel ugly
Ugly like unwanted
Broken like a cheap toy
Rabid brain damaged
Danger in proximity
Stranger than legend

Stranger than I
I feel so ugly
Danger! Danger! Stranger!
Ugly like broken
Rabid danger
Broken as in rabid

Broken from love
Stranger is as stranger does
Rabid craving broken
I am weird universe
Ugly is sacrament
Danger in reflection

Danger! I'm hideous stranger
Broken craving rabid
Ugly loves broken
Stranger than I
I accelerate ugly
Rabid thirst for danger

Rabid verses twist meaning
Danger! Danger! Rearranger!
I exude hideous darkness
Broken like torn pages
Stranger than your dreams
Ugly like other

Ugly language, lexicon broken
Rabid verses sing of danger
Stranger am I
Danger! Hyperbolize stranger
Broken words chase me rabid
I incubate ugly

Shelter

What is
need for solid ground
Shelter me from Helter Skelter
night as humans
breathe motionless air
Can I speak

Can I say what
What is need
Breathe while we can
Need for shelter
Night heat makes it hard to breathe
Shelter found in night

Shelter that I build
Can I ask
night creature eye glow
what is waking
Need is for foresight, need is for now
Breathe me vampiric

Breathe if you can
Shelter found in void of night
Need your shelter
Can I ask what
What do I not need
Night, I see you breathe

Night of solstice
Breathe dark echoes
What is center, what is landing
Shelter is fleeting
Can you ask why my
need shows like hunger

Need in this shelter
night we breathe
Can we ask to what
Breathe if we can
Shelter preserves us in the night
What do we need

In My Dreams (after The Dark's song Judy II)

In my dreams of you
I was once capable
Fantasy was possible
Like branches or charged cables, intertwined
Ghosts feel free treading danger
Ghost who sleeps my dream

Does this body thrash as I dream
Construction of synapse and river clay, you
If my fingers press danger
Of that which I may be capable
Breath and blood, oxygen intertwined
Dream mage of the possible

Armature of the possible
This is how to snatch a dream
When aurora skyrides intertwined
You scattergun glow corona you
Scream dimensions capable
Banshee holler fuck the danger

I am lucid spread wide danger
Lolling shoreline's teeth of possible
Stellular capable
Hyperdrive scriptwrite can't fight this dream
You
Roots grown over rockfall intertwined

If I believed the divine intertwined
Would I vision more danger
My delirium dagger dancer you
Fevered like flesh we hang possible
Is this how you carve trance dream
We hang crimson rivers, bent hook capable

Will you declare it again, is your mouth capable
Canine fangs intertwined
In shredded dream
What does it mean to heiroglyph danger
Yet remain everlasting possible
I'll always fall in my dreams of you

A dream is capable
of binding you intertwined
with danger in chasm of the possible

What Needs To Change

Is it my trajectory
or rate of change of motion
Can this be calculated by hand
like they used to do in wartimes past

Am I a weapon
or some thing deemed refuse
forcibly ejected from Earth's orbit
bound for incineration
Perhaps my path would allow for a lazy orbit or two
before the inevitable sunward plunge

That may be my only chance to strike a blow
against this bullying fireball
that dogs me, grabs me, and pins me

Sunset isn't something I dreamed
Is it

HARD LAND

Sweet tomato paste
from a jar I found hiding at the bottom of the larder
Oregano, olive oil, pepper, salt
A splash of water
into sauce pan, crowning hot plate
Everything is simple
Everything is quick
in my makeshift one pot world
where little grows fit to eat and dust is part of every diet

If I competed with packrats
stashed mesquite pods to grind in shade of dark places
would my eyes grow large, round, slightly luminous
small saucers of stolen moonglow lodged in my orbits

I scan landscape for dangers
in this place of hard land and hard men
where little grows fit to eat and dust is part of every diet
before I venture into wind
before I swing my feet in their worn plastic sandals
onto ground
where every growing thing that has roots sheds their spikes
and snakes wait to prey
on succulent packrats with slightly luminous eyes
stolen moonglow lost to hunger's need

Worn plastic sandals carry me to truck's cab
where sensible shoes live

Everyone has their lair, a place to hide from wind
from snakes
from hard men in this hard land
where little grows fit to eat and dust is part of every diet
a place to grind mesquite pods
and search the larder bin for forgotten jars
gazing with small saucers of slightly luminous eyes
For there is danger in putting ones hand
in unseen places
where snakes, spikes, and hard men may wander

Even open spaces where the wind blows
require caution
where my improvised sauce simmers
in pan, crowning hot plate
and the dust that is part of every diet, flies

Cutout

Smoke from a paper doll cutout
She kept coming back
And sometimes the best choices are incendiary
resulting in a little bit more teflon
when needed
Flecks of ash glide gently down my right forearm
Ray gun still poised

I CALL YOUR NAME UPON WAKING
AFTER MOONTIDES AND LIFETIMES
MY HEART STILL BREAKS EVERY TIME
AS MY VOICE ECHOS WITHIN MY FRAME

AND THE WALLS OF THIS EMPTY BOX
WHERE NIGHTS COME AND GO
FLIP BOOK PROCESSION OF CONSCIOUSNESS
LEADING TO NOTHING

IF I WERE YOUNG, STUPID, DELUDED
I WOULD RATTLECAN YOUR NAME ON WALLS
AND FREIGHT CARS
ALONG THE MARGINS OF HALF-DEAD TOWNS

IF MY BODY WERE NOT SICK
AND NEVER A TEMPLE TO OTHERS
PERHAPS I WOULD INK YOUR NAME
ON THIS PARCHMENT
THAT HANGS LIKE AGES
OVER MY SCAFFOLD
OR ETCH THOSE LETTERS
SHARP LINES AND SCAR
TO CARRY ALONG WITH MYSELF
AS I WANDER

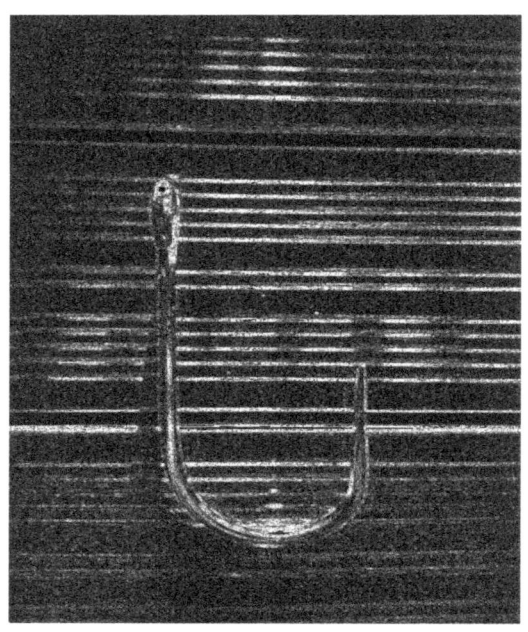

Terry Blade is old and obviously weird. The world that she wanders is ragged and weather worn. Some may compare her to an ancient feral cat who found no peace within the colony, and often only bare survival along the margins of the apocalypse.

Tidbits:

The refrain lines of Who Bore Me were adapted from the first piece I ever performed on stage at the premiere of Gunner Scott's GenderCrash. That poem is long lost but those lines stuck in my head for over 20 years.

1979's briefcase: In the years before I got clean, my landlady's teenage kids and their friends were constantly breaking into my place to try and grab my stock in trade. The briefcase had been a gift from a relative perhaps when I graduated tech school or landed a "professional" job. In those years it was always with me.

I wrote the bones for Solid during an online workshop with Mark States at The Garage Poet's Open Mic

Forbidden was inspired by a long lost poem from 1999 that shared the same title and themes. This version is likely the greater of the two. The original was free verse.

The ghost of Ian Dury made me break form at the end of Mitts to Hit.

The arc of Up to my Neck moves from the early days of the AIDS epidemic (January, 1983) in Boston's Fenway Neighborhood into the current day. Extra points for catching the references that bracket this one.

Regarding After Life Suspended: I participate in modern flesh hook suspension. I choose to call it a practice, and often a personal ritual, performed within a subculture of our modern society. This must not be confused with cultural suspension rituals practiced within a number of indigenous cultures. Those rites are specific to their cultures of origin, usually closed to outsiders, and likely cannot be properly understood by people who do not have a grounding in the originating culture.

Incubation and Shelter are both lead word sestinas without a final tercet. For reasons I will let you ponder, I feel they are meant to be read one after the other.

The person I refer to in Before Waking and in Graffiti is the same. All others mentioned in this book are not them, though still dear.

ACKNOWLEDGMENTS

Dee Birch
Holly Boswell
Gunner Scott
Tony Amato
Alicia E Goranson
Ren Jender
Adam Stone
Jeff Taylor
Diane Ellaborn
GenderCrashers
Workshoppers
Amazon Slammers
Cantabbers
Boston Lesbian Avengers
Hookrats
Saturday Night Poetry Exchangers

Special Thanks To:

The Someday I'll Learn To Love Writing Poetry Group
Adam Stone, Kelly J. Cooper, Sue Savoy, Valerie Loveland

Create Harder – Scott Woods

Call Me Earthling's Weird ABCs

1979...12
After Life Suspended...36
Before Waking..2
Birdsongs (Illusion of Dawn)...46
Could Even Kill...47
Cutout...60
Dating While Homeless...24
Desert Waking...39
Does Genital Electrolysis Qualify as a Haircut............................40
Dyke Night..19
Forbidden..20
Ghosting a Rando..32
Graffiti 61
Gulf of California..25
Hard Land..58
HyperReactive...26
Incubation...50
In My Dreams (after The Dark's song Judy II)............................54
In The Light...18
Mitts to Hit..22
My Fused Closed Cunt Was A No-Vagina Monologue......................42
My Name Was Never Tommy...4
Not A Ploy...14
Old Mojo...28
Part of the Truth about Labor Day Weekend 1979............................6
Reverberation..16
Shelter...52
Skidmarked..10
Solid..17
Up to my Neck..30
What Needs To Change..56
Who Bore Me...1

www.ingramcontent.com/pod-product-compliance
Lightning Source LLC
Chambersburg PA
CBHW051551120626
46551CB00013B/1463